SABINA

A SIX-SESSION VIDEO STUDY

the voice of the martyrs

SABINA GROUP STUDY PARTICIPANT'S GUIDE
Published by VOM Books
A division of The Voice of the Martyrs
1815 SE Bison Road
Bartlesville, OK 74006

is a registered trademark of The Voice of the Martyrs, Inc. and
may not be reproduced in whole or in part in any form without
written consent of The Voice of the Martyrs, Inc.

Scripture quotations are from the ESV® Bible (The Holy Bible, English
Standard Version®), Copyright © 2001 by Crossway, a publishing ministry
of Good News Publishers. Used by permission. All rights reserved.

ISBN: 978-0-88264-226-0
eISBN: 978-0-88264-238-3

Written by The Voice of the Martyrs with Stephen and Amanda Sorenson

Printed in China

202112p023b1

CONTENTS

Introduction

Few things capture our attention more than a great story.

Richard and Sabina Wurmbrand's story is the consummate love story—their love for one another, for God and for others—even for those that most would consider enemies. It is a love story that inspires each of us to obey God in loving others in order to win them to Christ.

Their story also shows us what daily obedience looks like for biblical disciples—a mature obedience that assesses risks and assumes there will be a price to pay in this world.

In the Sabina Group Study, you will meet seven women from around the world who, like Sabina, encountered great difficulty as they faithfully served Christ. The contributions of these women inspire each of us to realize that ordinary people, transformed by the love of God in Christ, can live obedient and fruitful lives.

Gracia Burnham

Martin and Gracia Burnham were serving as missionaries in the Philippines when they vacationed for a few days together to celebrate their anniversary. Those few days turned into a year in the jungle when they were kidnapped by radical Muslim terrorists. Martin was shot and killed during a rescue attempt; Gracia was also shot but survived to share the story of God's faithfulness in captivity.

Semse Aydin

Semse Aydin and her husband, Necati, were expecting a baby. Necati had been arrested for gospel work in Turkey, and now the couple had a decision to make. Would they continue advancing the gospel among their countrymen in spite of the risk of more persecution? Or would they choose a safer path for their now-growing family? Together, Necati and Semse made the decision: they would continue boldly in their Christian work. The decision led them to the city of Malatya, where Necati was murdered in 2007.

Rashin Soodmand

Rashin Soodmand was 13 years old when her father, Pastor Hossein Soodmand, was executed by the Iranian government for the crime of apostasy—leaving Islam to follow another faith. Her father's martyrdom did not frighten or deter Rashin from being obedient to Christ. It inspired her to follow in her father's footsteps through ministry.

Susanna Koh

On February 13, 2017, Susanna's husband, Pastor Raymond Koh, was abducted off the streets of Malaysia. Nearby security cameras captured the entire crime. Her husband hasn't been seen or heard from since; his car has never been found. It wasn't Raymond's first taste of persecution; he'd previously been mailed a box of bullets as a warning to stop his ministry.

Anita Smith

On December 5, 2013, Ronnie Smith was shot and killed in the Libyan city of Benghazi. Within days, Ronnie's wife, Anita, spoke on national television in the US about her love for the Libyan people and about forgiving her husband's murderers. She also gave interviews—in Arabic—that were broadcast throughout the Middle East.

Maryam Rostampour and Marziyeh Amirizadeh

Maryam and Marziyeh knew they were putting their lives on the line when they handed out thousands of New Testaments in Iranian neighborhoods, and they knew it when they shared the message of Jesus with their countrymen. Their bold witness for Christ would cost them: they spent 259 days in Iran's notorious Evin Prison.

This participant's guide explores, in depth, the opportunity we have to live as obedient biblical disciples. Both the Wurmbrands' story and the stories of these exemplary women will inspire you to take the next step of obedience, whatever it may be, and do so joyfully in spite of any price you may pay.

SUGGESTIONS FOR FACILITATING A GROUP OR CLASS

The video sessions are designed so that facilitators can choose one of three approaches. Prayerfully consider which approach best fits your group or class. You may even combine different approaches for different sessions.

Press play + pray

Play the video and lead your group to pray for our Christian brothers and sisters facing persecution. Pray as a group to be obedient and faithful witnesses at any cost.

Press play, two questions + pray

Play the video and lead your group to answer two questions:
- What captured your attention in what you saw? What inspired you in the video?
- What step is God asking you to take as a result of what inspired you?

Pray for our Christian brothers and sisters facing persecution. Pray as a group to be obedient and faithful witnesses at any cost.

Press play, discuss + pray

Play the video and facilitate a discussion using this participant's guide.

The participant's guide is designed for you to use
the sections titled "INTRODUCTION" and "VIDEO
DISCUSSION" for your group or class session.

Additional sections in the participant's guide will
benefit group or class participants in their individual
study through the week.

Don't feel pressured to cover every question offered in
the participant's guide.

Pray for our Christian brothers and sisters facing
persecution. Pray as a group to be obedient and faithful
witnesses at any cost.

Extended interviews can be viewed at vom.org/
SabinaExtras.

FAQ FOR GROUP OR
CLASS FACILITATORS

I have never facilitated a group or class before. Is this group study for me?

Thank you for your willingness to consider facilitating the *Sabina Group Study*. Remember that, with the Holy Spirit as instructor, you as the facilitator can create a meaningful experience for your group, class or family regardless of prior experience. This resource is designed for easy, accessible use.

What do you mean by "facilitate" the group or class?

Facilitators are fellow learners; they are not teachers or subject matter experts. Their primary role is to host the group or class and, using the resources provided, show the video and initiate the discussion.

Should our group view the film, *Sabina: Tortured for Christ, the Nazi Years,* prior to engaging the Sabina Group Study?

Viewing the film is not a requirement for your group to have a positive experience engaging with the Sabina Group Study. However, the film is a great introduction to the overall story and some groups have reported that holding an interest session for viewing the film prior to beginning the group study has encouraged participation.

Where can I learn more about persecuted Christians and The Voice of the Martyrs?

Visit vom.org in order to subscribe to our free monthly magazine, discover resources and learn more about Christians facing persecution in hostile areas and restricted nations.

Session 1

WE AREN'T BORN SAINTS

In those days we cared little about God. Nor very much about other people. We didn't want children. We wanted pleasure.

Sabina Wurmbrand, *Sabina: Tortured for Christ, the Nazi Years*

Introduction

When people talk about the "good life," what does that mean to you?

What motivates us to seek comfort, security, and rewards in this world so that we can achieve the "good life"?

Once we start pursuing the "good life" or believe we have achieved it, what makes us change what we value? What benefits, which we have gained for ourselves, do we give up?

Video Discussion

Watch the video for Session 1 and discuss the following questions with your class or group.

1. When we meet an inspiring person, especially someone who has lived an exemplary Christian life, what kind of assumptions do we make about that individual's life story?

What do we want to know about that person?

What questions does that person's story invite us to ask of ourselves?

2. Generally, people don't come to Christ through a one-time sales pitch. It usually takes a number of people, over a significant period of time, investing in the process to lead others to Christ. Additionally, as we participate in this process of sharing Christ faithfully, we should expect rejection. Although Richard Wurmbrand could not have realized it at the time, his illness, isolation, and the intervention of Christian Wölfkes launched him on a spiritual journey to experience Christ's love and to make it known to others. As a result, Richard and Sabina were on different spiritual trajectories.

What do you observe about Richard's growth in his faith as he considered Christ and shared his journey with Sabina, even though she openly opposed it?

Which characteristics of God's love do you see in Richard's interactions with Sabina?

Why do you think Richard was able to respond as he did to Sabina's rejection?

Would you find it easy or difficult to respond in a similar way?

3. Months into her traumatic experience as a hostage, what Gracia Burnham saw in herself deeply troubled her. When she faced the shocking realization that she felt hatred rather than love for her captors, she saw a version of herself she didn't want to believe existed. She struggled to believe that God—the God she had known about since she was a young child, who she knew gave himself to redeem her—really loved her. In what ways do you relate to Gracia's struggle?

How did Gracia and her husband, Martin, address her foundation-shaking thoughts about her identity as a faithful follower of Christ and her doubts about God's love for her?

How could their example help you face unsettling realizations about yourself that you may experience during your faith journey?

4. Even though God's Word reveals that what we call "righteousness" does not measure up to his righteousness (Isaiah 64:6), we may be tempted to assume that God offers salvation to those who are at least a little bit "good" or "deserving," or that it is easier for "good" people to receive the grace of God. The example of Jesus' interaction with Zacchaeus, the chief tax collector who presumably gained his wealth through dishonest collections, challenges these assumptions. Read Luke 19:1–10.

How socially and spiritually "acceptable" was Jesus' visit to Zacchaeus, and why?

How did that visit change Zacchaeus, and how did Jesus respond to that change?

Why did Jesus say he came to earth (v. 10), and what does that tell us about who "deserves" God's love and redemption?

How willing are you to love the "worst" of sinners and faithfully share the love you have received from Christ with them?

5. One of the characteristics of Richard and Sabina's life was that they were not complacent in developing their faith. They intentionally chose a path of obedience in studying God's Word and acting upon it, even when doing so put them at great risk. Gracia did the same when she recognized the discord in her heart during her captivity. She redirected her thoughts through prayer and by holding onto the truth of God's Word.

What are you facing today—circumstances, questions, doubts—that reveals God's work in you is not yet complete?

How eager are you to step forward in faithful obedience to share the love of Christ with the lost wherever God leads you?

Stepping Forward in the Power of God's Word

Reflect on these passages of Scripture throughout the week.

Christ Jesus is the one who died—more than that, who was raised—who is at the right hand of God, who indeed is interceding for us. Who shall separate us from the love of Christ? Shall tribulation, or distress, or persecution, or famine, or nakedness, or danger, or sword? As it is written,

"For your sake we are being killed all the day long; we are regarded as sheep to be slaughtered."

No, in all these things we are more than conquerors through him who loved us. For I am sure that neither death nor life, nor angels nor rulers, nor things present nor things to come, nor powers, nor height nor depth, nor anything else in all creation, will be able to separate us from the love of God in Christ Jesus our Lord.

Romans 8:34–39

Now the eleven disciples went to Galilee, to the mountain to which Jesus had directed them. And when they saw him they worshiped him, but some doubted. And Jesus came and said to them, "All authority in heaven and on earth has been given to me. Go therefore and make disciples of all nations, baptizing them in the name of the Father and of the Son and of the Holy Spirit, teaching them to observe all that I have commanded you. And behold, I am with you always, to the end of the age."

Matthew 28:16–20

For Additional Reflection

Sabina wasn't born an exemplary follower of Christ—no one is. Quite the opposite: she rejected the very idea of a god, even the God of her Jewish heritage.

This session's video opened with newlyweds Richard and Sabina happily discussing the highlights of their wedding day. They are wealthy, and the pursuit of success and pleasure means everything to them. They are focused on enjoying every moment to the fullest, fully embracing an atheistic and hedonistic life.

Sabina surely never imagined that her future would be characterized by life-threatening trials, brutal and humiliating imprisonment, and deep personal sacrifice, all made for the benefit of others and to honor the name of Christ—yet that is exactly what happened. Sabina's values and priorities in life changed so dramatically that instead of seeking fame and personal gain, she became willing to put herself in danger and risk ruthless persecution—even death—for the sake of the gospel and for those who are lost in sin.

How is such a dramatic change possible?

How does a person turn from selfishness to sacrifice?

Sabina and Richard Wurmbrand were drawn into a relationship with God. How did they step into faithful obedience and be transformed, by God's grace and power, into exemplary disciples of Christ?

1. Gracia and Martin quoted Scripture when Gracia began to question God's love during their captivity. The truth of Scripture anchored their thoughts in understanding God's nature and character in the midst of their trial. What do the following passages reveal about the character and depth of God's love?

Psalm 103:8–13—What does God's love compel him to do?

John 3:16–21—Why did God send his son into the world, and how does salvation through Christ impact our "works"?

Romans 5:6–8—What is most remarkable about Christ's sacrifice for us, and what does it reveal about God's love for us?

Ephesians 2:1–5—What is the evidence of someone who is "dead" in sin, and what did God's love do for us when we were at our worst?

2. When Richard and Sabina began investigating Christianity, they had no idea their highest priorities in life would be transformed. After all, what they valued and how they lived seemed perfectly normal for people who do not know or follow Jesus. The Bible, however, has always taught that true life goes far beyond what we see in this world. What true delight does Jeremiah 9:23–24 present in contrast to the world's pride in knowledge, power, and riches?

In what ways did the Wurmbrands invest in the process of growing in their knowledge of God and practicing virtues that delight the Lord?

Gracia could have focused on her circumstances as a hostage. She could have chosen the self-righteous path of pride, growing critical and grasping for what she needed and deserved in life. What path did she choose instead, and what about it was rewarding?

3. A personal relationship with Jesus changes everything. We see it in the story of Zacchaeus. We see it in the lives of Richard and Sabina. They were utterly lost, apart from God, pursuing the pleasures and riches of the temporary world.

How does the Apostle Paul describe the reason for the change we experience when we meet Jesus, and what is the outcome of that change? Read 2 Corinthians 5:14–15.

My Next Step—Making It Personal

During World War II and its aftermath, many Romanians suffered brutal persecution under the Nazi regime and later under the Russian Communists. Richard and Sabina were among those who were persecuted by the Nazis and then by the Communists. Yet their newfound relationship with Jesus motivated them to share with others the love God had shown them—including their most dangerous enemies.

Sabina helped hide retreating Nazi soldiers in order to protect them from death at the hands of the Russians. This was an act of sacrificial love that is impossible to comprehend from a human perspective. Even one of the soldiers she protected couldn't understand why she would do it and admitted that he would never do the same for her.

Read John 10:27–29, Romans 8:34–39, and Galatians 2:20, and discuss the motivation provided for a follower of Christ Jesus to live a life of sacrifice.

Think about ways God has shown his love to you. How does that motivate you to share his love with others?

No matter who we are, what we have done, how much we have opposed God's work in our lives, or where we are in our faith journey, God is rich in mercy. He loves us relentlessly. Even when we were unrepentant sinners, God sent Jesus as the perfect sacrifice to redeem us. God also continues to invest in our spiritual development. In Ephesians 2:4–10, the Apostle Paul says,

> *But God, being rich in mercy, because of the great love with which he loved us, even when we were dead in our trespasses, made us alive together with Christ—by grace you have been saved—and raised us up with him and seated us with him in the heavenly places in Christ Jesus, so that in the coming ages he might show the immeasurable riches of his grace in kindness toward us in Christ Jesus. For by grace you have been saved through faith. And this is not your own doing; it is the gift of God, not a result of works, so that no one may boast. For we are his workmanship, created in Christ Jesus for good works, which God prepared beforehand, that we should walk in them.*

We are the workmanship of God. "Workmanship" describes the hard labor and skillful crafting that produces a high-quality result. Workmanship is a process that requires time and commitment. Before we come to Christ, we are not saints in any way. We are sinners in need of divine transformation. Through his grace and power, God is faithful to work in us and bring us to completion in order to accomplish the good works he has ordained for us to do.

Which specific areas of your lifestyle and spiritual character will you pray for God to complete in you?

How diligently do you cooperate with God's continued workmanship in your life even when it takes place under difficult circumstances?

Session 2

"I Don't Want to Waste My Life"

Love is patient and kind; love does not envy or boast; it is not arrogant or rude. It does not insist on its own way; it is not irritable or resentful; it does not rejoice at wrongdoing, but rejoices with the truth. Love bears all things, believes all things, hopes all things, endures all things. Love never ends.

1 Corinthians 13:4–8

Introduction

When have you taken time to really think about your life—where it is headed, what you value and how you want life to be different? And what impact did that time of introspection and evaluation have on who you are today?

Think about ways to keep your focus on what is truly important in life. Consider this when your life is good and when you face difficulties or challenging situations.

Video Discussion

Watch the video for Session 2 and discuss the following questions with your class or group.

1. What a change of pace Richard experienced when he was diagnosed with tuberculosis! His busy life was over: no more buying and selling stocks, no more discussions with influential friends, no more theater, no more parties. Richard had more free time than ever before, but it wasn't exactly leisure time. What impact did this extended time—alone and isolated from his normal life—have on him?

2. Richard experienced more than isolation; he faced an intimidating 50/50 survival rate. When he learned that he might not survive, what did he conclude about his life?

How did Sabina respond to his emphatic statement about living what he called a "wasted life"?

How do you think each of them at that time would define or characterize a "wasted life"?

What are you pursuing in your own life? Is it leading toward a "wasted life" or a fruitful life? How do you know?

3. Semse and Necati faced danger and opposition from the moment they began their journey as followers of Christ. They met discreetly every week for months, never knowing if their activity might be discovered. When Necati told his family of his new life in Christ, they responded to Semse with hatred and false accusations and rejected Necati as if he were dead. Despite the opposition and

danger, the couple continued to introduce people to Jesus wherever they went.

What motivated and sustained them to so eagerly and faithfully "take Jesus" with them even into the most hostile region of eastern Turkey?

How do you think they reached the point where they could pray that they would be faithful unto death?

4. First Corinthians 13 is a familiar Bible passage, often quoted during wedding ceremonies as guidance for a loving marriage, but its meaning holds more significance. Let's look closely to see how God's kind of love results in living a life that will not be wasted.

Read 1 Corinthians 13:4–8 aloud. Instead of viewing this passage through the lens of marriage, as we often do, hear it as a description of how graciously God loves us, even before we know him and when we reject or oppose him.

What does knowing God loves you like this mean to you? How does it feel?

How important is it to your relationship with God to experience him as patient and kind rather than rude, arrogant, irritable, or resentful toward you?

What did God bear, believe, hope, and endure in order to win your heart?

How would your response to God have been different if he had decided you were unreachable, hopeless, and not worth his time?

Read 1 Corinthians 13:4–8 again. This time, hear it as a description of how God intends us, his followers, to approach those who are lost so that we may share the love and truth of Christ with them.

Rejection, when we endeavor to share God's love with those who do not yet know him, is difficult. When we are bullied, slandered, physically harmed, denied jobs, shut out of relationships, or mocked, becoming irritated, resentful, or rude in return is a natural reponse. What perspective and attitudes can help us respond with love?

In what ways are some of our approaches to the lost actually arrogant, insistent, and boastful? What prompts us to take such an approach?

How do we harm the message of God's unquenchable love if we—God's messengers—are impatient, irritable, arrogant, unkind, or rude to people who need to know and experience it?

What do we need to bear, believe, hope, and endure in order to share the love of Jesus with those who do not know him? What may be the consequences if we fail to do so?

5. Semse lived in the country of Turkey, where Islam is not only the predominant religion, but also the identity of its citizens. To be Turkish is to be Muslim. As an exemplary biblical disciple, Semse rejected this nationalistic identity and embraced her true identity in Christ. She did so at great risk and counted the cost of living as a stranger and alien in her own country. Semse knew who she was—*whose* she was—and that understanding propelled her to turn away from valuing her temporary identity in this world over her identity in Christ.

How might Semse have behaved differently if she had considered her national identity more valuable than her identity in Christ?

Read Colossians 3:1–3. How do these verses inform your view of your identity in Christ?

What are some earthly things believers may pursue that distract them from living obediently for Christ?

How does pursuing these earthly things lead us to living a wasted life?

When Paul writes, "For you have died, and your life is hidden with Christ in God," how do these words free you from grasping at and pursuing any earthly distractions?

Stepping Forward in the Power of God's Word

Reflect on these passages of Scripture throughout the week.

> Beloved, let us love one another, for love is from God, and whoever loves has been born of God and knows God. Anyone who does not love does not know God, because God is love. In this the love of God was made manifest among us, that God sent his only Son into the world, so that we might live through him. In this is love, not that we have loved God but that he loved us and sent his Son to be the propitiation for our sins. Beloved, if God so loved us, we also ought to love one another. No one has ever seen God; if we love one another, God abides in us and his love is perfected in us.
>
> 1 John 4:7–12

> But we have this treasure in jars of clay, to show that the surpassing power belongs to God and not to us. We are afflicted in every way, but not crushed; perplexed, but not driven to despair; persecuted, but not forsaken; struck down, but not

destroyed; always carrying in the body the death of Jesus, so that the life of Jesus may also be manifested in our bodies. For we who live are always being given over to death for Jesus' sake, so that the life of Jesus also may be manifested in our mortal flesh.

2 Corinthians 4:7–11

For Additional Reflection

Most of us know what we want our lives to look like. We may want a nice house in a good neighborhood with plenty of friends. We may want an enjoyable job that allows us the leisure we want when we want it. We may want to be active in a vibrant church community. We make plans, take the steps, and expect life to unfold just the way we think it should.

But life doesn't always work out that way. Businesses fail; homes disappear in floods or fires; injuries and illness make "normal" life impossible; friends and family members die; circumstances beyond our control change. Life as we know it and want it to be can be interrupted, and such interruptions are often difficult, sometimes devastating. God, however, is sovereign and loving. What we view as interruptions, God views as investment. In God's hands, interruptions to our life story are never outside of his knowledge.

When God allows an interruption to our life story, another one is about to begin.

- Consider Esther. What a tragedy to lose both parents! Taken in by her uncle Mordecai, she later became the wife of King Ahasuerus (Xerxes), ruler of the Persian Empire. God used her influence with the king to save the Jewish people, her people, from genocide (Esther 1–10).

- Joseph, his father's favored son, was sold as a slave and imprisoned but eventually became second only to Pharaoh in Egypt (Genesis 37–47). God elevated his status not only to save Egypt from famine but also to preserve Joseph's entire family—even the brothers who betrayed him.

- Mary, a virgin engaged to be married, saw her life story shatter when, through the power of God, she became the mother of Jesus (Luke 1:26–56).

- And let's not forget Saul, whose driving goal was to serve God by tracking down and arresting followers of Christ (Acts 9:1–19)! After he encountered Jesus, Saul's life purpose turned around. Rather than destroying the early church, he took the name of Christ to both Jews and Gentiles and established churches throughout the Roman Empire.

In God's hands, Richard and Sabina's interrupted life led to a new life that would not be wasted but would yield eternal rewards. Let's examine who we are in Christ and consider our commitment to becoming biblical disciples who live lives that are not wasted.

1. As biblical disciples, each of us has the mission of sharing God's love with the lost. Semse told Necati, in a seemingly random meeting on the bus, "I am not a missionary, but a mail delivery person, and I have a letter from your heavenly Father for you."

2 Corinthians 5:17–21 helps us understand how important it is it to pursue that mission and what enables and motivates us to do so.

How does reconciliation to God bring about a dramatic change in our identity (v. 17)?

What ministry and message has God entrusted to those who have been reconciled to God through the shed blood of Jesus Christ (vv. 18–19)?

What, then, is the role, mission, and privilege of everyone who follows Jesus (vv. 20–21)?

What clear command did Jesus give to his disciples regarding the ministry and message of reconciliation through him? Read Matthew 28:19–20.

2. The Wurmbrands and Necati may have been labeled "unreachable" by Christians. However, we must remember that, despite appearances, no one, absolutely no one, is beyond the reach of God's love and redemption. Mark 5:1–20 (see also Luke 8:26–39) tells the story of Jesus' encounter with a man who lived in the Gentile territory across the Sea of Galilee from Capernaum.

How had this man shown himself to be unreachable (Mark 5:2–5)?

In what ways did Jesus show his love for this man, and what indicates that the man recognized that love (Mark 5:6–13)?

How well was Jesus received by the local community after he healed the man (Mark 5:14–17)?

· What "assignment" did Jesus give to the man (Mark 5:18–19), and how does it compare to the assignment that Jesus gives to everyone who follows him?

How did the man respond to Jesus' command (Mark 5:20)?

3. Semse and Necati's story is a story of love—love for Christ, love for the lost, and love for one another. It is also a story about the difficulty of rejection, opposition, and real danger that a faithful witness for Christ may face. Semse and Necati recognized themselves to be bearers of Christ to everyone they met. In what ways did their lives reflect the message of 2 Corinthians 2:14–17?

What did Semse know and believe about God's love that helped her to view Necati's martyrdom as a victory? Read 1 John 5:1–4.

What are you facing in life that, like Semse, might change your perspective if you saw through God's eyes?

My Next Step—Making it Personal

At the beginning of this session, we saw a Sabina who was comfortable with her self-absorbed life. She was appalled and offended when her husband, Richard, suggested that the life they lived was a wasted life. Despite her objections, Richard continued on his spiritual journey to discover Christ and soon surrendered his heart and life to serving him. Patiently and tenderly, he bore all of Sabina's protests and insults until she, too, submitted her heart to the truth of Christ's love for her. From that time on, they both knew they belonged to God and determined in their hearts to serve him fully, no matter what the cost.

The cost of faithfully serving Christ in Romania under Nazi occupation, and later under Communist rule, was steep. After years of imprisonment for her faith, Sabina was transferred to a state pig farm. Of that experience, she writes:

> The years had been hard, but this was the hardest of all. Food was at starvation level. We dragged ourselves from our beds at 5 a.m., still wearing the filthy rags in which we had lain down, and went out into the cold and darkness to feed the pigs.
>
> The sties were ankle-deep in liquid filth—the one substance that never froze. A vile, nauseating stench hung about the body and hair. The very

gruel we slopped up with our wooden spoons reeked of it....

The meaning fell away from things. Death stared me in the face. The whole world was made of tears and despair as never before and a cry rose from my heart: "My God, my God, why have you forsaken me?"

Trying to clean their sties was as hopeless as trying to clean the world. Each day we started afresh, wet, hungry and half dead, to carry away in barrows the mountains of filth.

I knew there was no hope for me, nor for the world, and expected only to die.

And perhaps, in a psychological condition such as this, I should not have survived for long. But happily it did not last for many weeks. I am convinced that the Lord heard my prayers and took me out according to his plan. I had only to learn a very deep lesson, to drink the cup to its bitterest dregs; and now I am thankful that I passed through this hard school, which teaches you the highest love, love toward God, even when he gives nothing but suffering.

The Pastor's Wife

Despite the bitter suffering and losses Sabina experienced during her time of imprisonment and forced labor, she recognized that even this part of her life was not wasted. Through it, her love for God grew deeper than she had ever imagined. Suffering for the cause of Christ is real. It can be painful beyond what we can imagine. Yet suffering is part of the journey.

God's Word warns, prepares, strengthens, and comforts every disciple for the reality of suffering for Christ. Repeatedly, New Testament writers, themselves faithful witnesses of Christ who experienced suffering and martyrdom, offer encouragement to their fellow believers. Consider these passages from 1 Peter:

> *Beloved, do not be surprised at the fiery trial when it comes upon you to test you, as though something strange were happening to you. But rejoice insofar as you share Christ's sufferings, that you may also rejoice and be glad when his glory is revealed. If you are insulted for the name of Christ, you are blessed, because the Spirit of glory and of God rests upon you.... Therefore let those who suffer according to God's will entrust their souls to a faithful Creator while doing good.*
>
> 1 Peter 4:12–14, 19

How challenging is it for you to view suffering as a normal, rather than abnormal, part of your faith journey?

In what ways might you need to rethink your perspective, values, and priorities in order to see suffering and insults for the name of Christ as signs of blessing and reasons to rejoice?

Humble yourselves, therefore, under the mighty hand of God so that at the proper time he may exalt you, casting all your anxieties on him, because he cares for you. Be sober-minded; be watchful. Your adversary the devil prowls around like a roaring lion, seeking someone to devour. Resist him, firm in your faith, knowing that the same kinds of suffering are being experienced by your brotherhood throughout the world. And after you have suffered a little while, the God of all grace, who has called you to his eternal glory in Christ, will himself restore, confirm, strengthen, and establish you. To him be the dominion forever and ever. Amen.

1 Peter 5:6–11

What comfort and encouragement do you find in God's love and faithfulness that care for you in the midst of suffering?

How ready or resistant are you to entrusting your mind, body, soul, and future into the hands of your Creator?

Session 3

THE JOURNEY TOWARD DISCIPLESHIP

I am a follower of the Great Shepherd of the sheep, our Lord Jesus Christ, and I am ready to sacrifice my soul for my sheep. For me to escape from this persecution would cause the hearts of my flock to become cold and weak. I never want to be a bad example for them. So I am ready to go to prison again, and if necessary to give my life.

Pastor Hossein Soodmand, Iran

Introduction

When we talk with other Christians about our discipleship journey, we may discuss a variety of topics—practicing spiritual disciplines, evangelism, Bible studies, and more—but when was the last time you had a serious conversation about *obedience*, particularly obedience that may prove costly?

Why do you think obedience is an unpopular topic for many Christians to discuss?

What might compel us to live obediently and sacrificially to serve Christ and his kingdom?

Let's think specifically about what wholehearted obedience to Christ might look like in your daily faith journey. How are you disobedient at home, at work, at leisure, or in service to others?

What different choices might you make at home, at work, at leisure, or in your service to others? What would those choices cost you?

How would you answer if someone asked you, "What difference does it make in your life to be a Christian? Does a Christian have to live life by certain rules or in a certain way?"

Would Christians you know answer differently than you?

How do you think Richard and Sabina would answer these questions?

How do you think Pastor Soodman and his daughter, Rashin, might answer these questions?

Video Discussion

Watch the video for Session 3 and discuss with your class or group the following questions.

1. Richard and Sabina were relatively new Christians when the Nazi occupation dramatically changed life in Romania. As you

viewed the checkpoint scene, what did you realize about the seriousness of their situation due to their official designation as Jews?

Do you think they had prepared to make the decision they chose? Explain your answer.

Are you and other Christians you know prepared to live out your faith under the threat of difficult, and perhaps dangerous, challenges?

2. Pastor Soodmand's ministry in one of Iran's most intensely faithful Muslim cities was noticed not only by the religious police but also by ordinary people. What did people who knew nothing about Christ recognize about the "church in the basement" and the pastor who established it? How did they respond?

After the police locked his church door, why did Pastor Soodmand risk continuing his ministry?

How did the pastor's ministry impact his local community and elsewhere?

3. During the early days of Richard's faith journey, Sabina wanted nothing to do with Christianity, much less commit herself to becoming a disciple of Jesus. Because Richard loved her dearly, he patiently and persistently introduced her to the truth of the gospel. Richard was not a mature Christian at this point; he was simply one step ahead of his wife. Yet he acted in obedience to share what he was learning.

> What did you learn, from his example, about the process of sharing the gospel message with others?

4. By the time Pastor Soodmand was arrested, his daughter, Rashin, had observed him and learned from him for many years. His execution and the killings of other pastors that followed was a terrible shock to her and her family.

> What did she learn about the Christian faith through what she witnessed, and how did she respond?

Today, Rashin says she is proud of how her father persisted in choosing Christ, no matter how great the cost. She saw firsthand how the enemy, Satan, could not stop the work of God when his people chose to obey their calling. Unknown followers of Christ throughout the world are doing the same, choosing to obey Christ, pay a price, and bear fruit for eternity.

What different choices do we and other Christians need to make in order to join in God's work of redemption that is occurring all around the world?

5. Learning how to walk out our commitment to Christ faithfully is a serious matter. Who has provided examples of obedient, sacrificial faith that stand out and encourage you to carry on? Examples could be from Scripture, the stories of exemplary Christians, or believers you have known personally.

The specific choices we make on our faith journey ultimately depend on one choice: "Will I obey Christ's calling on my life and choose to serve his purposes above all else, or will I choose to serve myself and serve the purposes of the enemy?"

How do the examples you named above help you choose obedience to Christ above all else?

Stepping Forward in the Power of God's Word

Reflect on these passages of Scripture throughout the week.

> But the steadfast love of the LORD is from ever-
> lasting to everlasting on those who fear him, and
> his righteousness to children's children, to those
> who keep his covenant and remember to do his
> commandments.
>
> Psalm 103:17–18

> My little children, I am writing these things to
> you so that you may not sin. But if anyone does
> sin, we have an advocate with the Father, Jesus
> Christ the righteous. He is the propitiation for
> our sins, and not for ours only but also for the
> sins of the whole world. And by this we know
> that we have come to know him, if we keep his
> commandments. Whoever says "I know him" but
> does not keep his commandments is a liar, and
> the truth is not in him, but whoever keeps his
> word, in him truly the love of God is perfected.
> By this we may know that we are in him: whoever

says he abides in him ought to walk in the same
way in which he walked.

1 John 2:1–6

For Additional Reflection

Growing in our faith doesn't happen automatically. There is no
"spiritual growth button" for becoming an exemplary servant of
Christ. Deep faith and powerful witness for Christ come through
intentional sacrificial choices to obey and serve him above all else.

Every opportunity we encounter to serve Christ comes with a
price. We must weigh the cost and make our choice. Biblical disciples obey God regardless of the cost because he is Lord over all.

How we can learn to live out our faith by choosing to obey
and serve God faithfully, no matter the cost?

1. Jesus Christ our Lord chose to obey God rather than serve
any other interest or purpose. We see evidence of such choices
throughout his life, and he made no greater choice than on the
night before his crucifixion. Read Luke 22:39–46.

Jesus knew all too well what the next hours would bring. He knew the physical suffering, the unbearable separation from his Father when he bore on himself the sins of the world, and the sorrow suffered by those who knew and loved him. What did he ask God to do, and on what important condition did he make his request?

Even when facing humiliation, torture, and death, what did Jesus recognize—and choose—as the highest priority?

In what ways does Jesus' example of faithful obedience impact the choices you make on your faith journey?

2. When the apostles taught in the temple, crowds of people became believers. Acts 5:12–42 reveals how the apostles' witness caused trouble for Jerusalem's religious leaders. To end the apostles' teaching, the high priest imprisoned them—but that's when the story gets more interesting. Read Acts 5:19–26.

What happened during the night? How did the apostles respond to the opportunity God created for them to continue their witness in the temple courts?

How did these events impact those who opposed the apostles?

Read Acts 5:27–33.

How did the apostles' obedience to continue teaching impact those in Jerusalem?

What fundamental choice had the apostles made that motivated their persistent witness?

How essential is that same choice in the lives of biblical disciples today?

To what extent do you think the apostles had counted the cost and assessed the risk they faced from the high priest and the council?

Read Acts 5:38–39.

Although some council members wanted the apostles killed, what advice did they eventually heed?

Read Acts 5:40–42.

What did the apostles suffer for continuing to testify about Jesus in the temple, and how did they respond?

What does their response indicate about their love for their Savior and their commitment to obey Christ, no matter what?

In what way does the apostles' example of faithful obedience challenge you to reconsider your commitment to obey God? What might such commitment require of you?

Even though the authorities locked the doors to his church, people still came to Pastor Soodmand asking questions about God. They learned about Jesus and submitted their hearts to him. They worshiped and his church grew.

What similarities do you recognize in Pastor Soodmand's and the apostles' commitment to continue teaching and answering questions about Jesus?

3. We don't come to Christ knowing exactly what our faith journey will require of us, nor do we come equipped to make the ultimate sacrifice in obedience to him. We learn these things by knowing God's Word, considering the examples of faithfulness set before us, and choosing to obey God's commands one step at a time. Read Ephesians 5:1–2; Philippians 2:1–13; and 2 Timothy 1:8–12. If we desire to walk out our faith sacrificially, in obedience to Christ, what must we understand about…

…what Jesus did to redeem us?

…our holy calling as his disciples?

…the example he set for us to follow?

4. Christians around the world—not unlike the Wurmbrands and Pastor Soodmand—are obediently walking out their faith and joyfully paying a price that will bear fruit for eternity.

Read James 1:22–25.

What essential step must we take in order to walk out our faith in a similar manner and join the global body of Christ in bringing honor to God's name?

How does the faithful obedience of Pastor Soodmand, Rashin and the Wurmbrands inspire you to walk out your faith?

My Next Step—Making it Personal

If we are committed to following Christ, the daily choices we make are more significant than we realize. Our choices not only make an impact at the time but also influence the future. Our choices become our legacy, the example of Christian living that we leave behind.

Rashin remembers her father as a loving pastor who faithfully shared Jesus and God's love to others. Many believed his testimony, and his life was taken because of his faithfulness. Can you imagine how you, as a young teenager, might have responded if your father had been abducted without warning and executed by the government because he shared the truth about God? Try to imagine the chilling shock when other pastors Rashin knew, the very ones who helped care for her family, were kidnapped, imprisoned, and killed as well.

How would these circumstances have affected your faith?

To what extent would you have questioned God's love for you? Would you have wanted to continue growing in your faith?

Rashin did not abandon her faith when her father was killed. Instead, she was proud of her father's choices and the example of faithful obedience he had left behind. Inspired by him, she wrote a letter to God, promising to carry on the faith and legacy her father passed on to her. We don't know the influence our faith legacy may have in the future, but considering it is wise. As you read the following questions, consider how the examples in the Scripture passages influence your faith journey.

In what ways did Pastor Soodmand's example to shepherd the flock, whom God had placed under his care, reflect the exhortation in 1 Peter 5:2–3?

In John 13:12–17, Jesus presented himself and his own actions as an example for his disciples. What did he want them to remember and put into practice?

What legacy of faithfulness and endurance has Jesus left for us to follow? Read Hebrews 12:1–3.

In what ways does 1 Peter 2:21–25 present Jesus as an example for us to follow?

How did the faithfulness of the Thessalonian believers impact the ministry of the gospel in their community? Read 1 Thessalonians 1:4–8.

Rashin shared a vital perspective when she spoke about the influence of her father's legacy and the example of faithful obedience he left behind. She also shared her insightful perspective on how we can obey Christ faithfully when the cost is high. She said she could not have survived the time following her father's execution without God's presence, love, grace, and mercy—and she can still feel God's presence with her as she continues her faith journey. We are not walking this journey of obedience alone. Take some time to consider God's faithfulness to those who obey his commands:

Who shall separate us from the love of Christ? Shall tribulation, or distress, or persecution, or famine, or nakedness, or danger, or sword? As it is written,

"For your sake we are being killed all the day long; we are regarded as sheep to be slaughtered."

No, in all these things we are more than conquerors through him who loved us. For I am sure that neither death nor life, nor angels nor rulers, nor things present nor things to come, nor powers, nor height nor depth, nor anything else in all creation, will be able to separate us from the love of God in Christ Jesus our Lord.

Romans 8:35–39

Blessed be the God and Father of our Lord Jesus Christ, the Father of mercies and God of all comfort, who comforts us in all our affliction, so that we may be able to comfort those who are in any affliction, with the comfort with which we ourselves are comforted by God. For as we share abundantly in Christ's sufferings, so through Christ we share abundantly in comfort too.

2 Corinthians 1:3–5

Do not be anxious about anything, but in everything by prayer and supplication with thanksgiving let your requests be made known to God. And the peace of God, which surpasses all understanding, will guard your hearts and your minds in Christ Jesus.

Philippians 4:6–7

Since then we have a great high priest who has passed through the heavens, Jesus, the Son of God, let us hold fast our confession. For we do not have a high priest who is unable to sympathize with our weaknesses, but one who in every respect has been tempted as we are, yet without sin. Let us then with confidence draw near to the throne of grace, that we may receive mercy and find grace to help in time of need.

Hebrews 4:14–16

Each one of us will face challenges and choices on our faith journey. No matter what circumstances we may be called to endure, our loving God promises his presence, grace, and mercy to sustain us.

Today, what choices face you in your faith journey?

As you are embraced by God's love, surrounded by his grace and mercy, and unseparated from his presence, what commitment are you willing to make to God about how you will live out your faith this day?

Session 4

NECESSARY RISK

I appeal to you therefore, brothers, by the mercies of God, to present your bodies as a living sacrifice, holy and acceptable to God, which is your spiritual worship. Do not be conformed to this world, but be transformed by the renewal of your mind, that by testing you may discern what is the will of God, what is good and acceptable and perfect.

Romans 12:1–2

Introduction

When we discuss biblical discipleship, we may talk about "taking up our cross," "suffering for the cause of Christ," or being "a living sacrifice."

How do you interpret these phrases? What do such actions involve?

When we suffer for the sake of Christ, what is our expectation for God to demonstrate his love and care for us? Why?

When we are serious about living out our faith as biblical disciples and begin to consider the cost of obedience to Christ—the sacrifices, hardship, and pain we may have to endure—what emotions might we feel?

To what extent do these emotions influence our response to Christ's calling?

When our emotions tug at us to deny, run away, or disengage from obeying Christ's calling, what can help us stay focused on serving him faithfully?

Video Discussion

Watch the video for Session 4 and discuss the following questions with your class or group.

1. Many of us think that risk assessment helps us prioritize and avoid whatever might put us at risk. How does our perspective change when we turn risk assessment on its head and view it as prioritizing the risks that are worth the price?

For someone who is committed to following Christ, what is most worthy in life?

Which specific risks and costs have you determined are worth bearing because Christ is worthy?

2. Like the Wurmbrands and the Kohs, biblical disciples are opposed, abused, imprisoned, abducted, and even killed for the activity of their faith birthed by their belief in Christ. Seeing things God's way and thinking God's thoughts give biblical Christians the ability to take steps of obedience, no matter the price they will pay. They know the cost is real, but they overcome any fear by anchoring their lives in God's Word and through abiding in Christ day by day.

Which key spiritual discipline did both couples recognize as essential preparation for being a living sacrifice for Christ?

Scripture memory + faith

Why is knowing God's Word so important in the life of a biblical disciple? What does it accomplish in the heart, mind, and life of a faithful follower of Jesus?

Scripture is literally the most powerful thing ♡

★ 2 Tim 3:9 ★

Susanna Koh talked about God receiving the glory for whatever we sacrifice for him and mentioned that he does a "deep work" in our lives to make that possible. What do you think she meant by that statement? What brings about a "deep work" in our lives?

Suffering brings about that deep work

3. When Richard and Sabina became Christians, they prayed that God would give them a cross to bear. Rather than running from persecution, they recognized that sharing in Christ's suffering was the calling of biblical disciples. The idea of taking up our cross and following Jesus is antithetical to everything the world presents as worthy (Luke 9:23–25). To Jesus' disciples, it must have been horrifying. They understood in a way we can't imagine what it meant to bear a cross and die to self.

Why is Christ worthy of this extreme sacrifice? Read Revelation 5:9–12.

According to Romans 12:1–2, what kind of worship is Christ worthy to receive from those of us who would follow him?

Being a living sacrifice by taking up our cross daily requires humility, trust, and vulnerability in our relationship with God. How would practicing these characteristics daily align our thinking with God's will and transform our understanding of what is good, perfect, and acceptable?

Philippians 2:5–8 provides insight into the character of Christ and his sacrifice on the cross for us.

What do you learn from this passage about why obediently taking up our cross and following Jesus transform us into biblical disciples?

4. In Luke 21:12–19, Jesus speaks about what his followers will face because of him. Read this passage as if Jesus is speaking directly to you.

How do you assess the risk of being persecuted for Christ's sake as described in this passage?

How frightened would you be if brought before powerful authorities for questioning?

What would give you the peace and confidence to view such circumstances as opportunities to witness for Christ and to wait for God to speak through you?

Betrayal, especially by loved ones and friends, can be a bitter trial. How do you count the cost of being hated or betrayed, and what would make such a sacrifice worthwhile for you?

What hope does Christ alone provide for enduring such circumstances, and to what extent is it sufficient for you?

As you count the cost of biblical discipleship, which sacrifices are most costly—most difficult for you to bear?

What are you afraid of losing if you risk everything to serve your Lord and Savior? What will you lose if you don't take the risk?

Stepping Forward in the Power of God's Word

Reflect on these passages of Scripture throughout the week.

Now may our Lord Jesus Christ himself, and God our Father, who loved us and gave us eternal comfort and good hope through grace, comfort your hearts and establish them in every good work and word.

2 Thessalonians 2:16–17

Now from Miletus he [Paul] sent to Ephesus and called the elders of the church to come to him. And when they came to him, he said to them:

"You yourselves know how I lived among you the whole time from the first day that I set foot in Asia, serving the Lord with all humility and with tears and with trials that happened to me through the plots of the Jews; how I did not shrink from declaring to you anything that was profitable, and teaching you in public and from house to house, testifying both to Jews and to Greeks of repentance toward God and of faith in our Lord Jesus Christ. And now, behold, I am going to Jerusalem, constrained by the Spirit, not knowing what will happen to me there, except that the Holy Spirit testifies to me in every city that imprisonment and afflictions await me. But I do not account my life of any value nor as precious to myself, if only I may finish my course

and the ministry that I received from the Lord
Jesus, to testify to the gospel of the grace of God."

Acts 20:17–24

For Additional Reflection

During our previous study session, we began exploring the role
obedience plays in our growth as biblical disciples. We considered
Jesus' faithful obedience, even submitting to death on the cross,
as our example. We saw his disciples joyfully follow his command
to teach and tell others about him even though they suffered at
the hands of powerful people who wanted to silence them. We
read repeated exhortations by the apostles for believers to follow
Christ's example and faithfully fulfill the calling of Christ through
their suffering, sacrifice, and endurance.

Faithful obedience that leads to exemplary biblical discipleship is more than doing the right actions for the right reasons.
It is about how we become who we become. Obedience is the
process by which our hearts grow into alignment with God's heart
so that we begin to see the world as he sees it and love the lost as he
loves them. Faithful obedience is transformational: When we, as
faithful servants who will risk everything for Christ, accept Christ's
Lordship because he alone is worthy of such a sacrifice of love, we
are shaped into "new creatures."

1. Before Jesus left his disciples, he clearly stated their future mission (Matthew 28:19–20): "Go therefore and make disciples of all nations, baptizing them in the name of the Father and of the Son and of the Holy Spirit, teaching them to observe all that I have commanded you." What else did Jesus teach in order to prepare his disciples for what would happen to him? Read Luke 9:22–26 (see also Mark 8:31–38; Mark 10:32–34).

In order to help his disciples understand the personal sacrifices that following him would require, what specific things did Jesus say they needed to do?

What risks did they face and how great a price would they have to pay in order to accomplish what Jesus required?

In what ways did Jesus present a change in perspective for his followers?

2. It was hard enough for Jesus' disciples to comprehend what would happen to him, much less what would happen to them

if they followed him and testified of his love and forgiveness. Throughout his ministry, how did Jesus prepare his disciples for a life of sacrifice? Read the following: Matthew 5:10–12; 10:37–39; Luke 14:27–30, 33; John 15:18–21.

> Which of these instructions and warnings must we recognize and take to heart if we are committed to becoming biblical disciples today?

> How might Jesus' warnings be evident in the world we live in, and in what specific ways can we faithfully obey his instructions and fulfill our calling?

> Why is it important that we count the cost of walking out our faith as biblical disciples?

3. As we study the role of obedience in the life of biblical disciples, it is important that we not lose sight of our motivation for obeying God's commands—which is not just the actions we take. Read John 14:15, 18–24. Why is it important to keep God's commandments?

What does our obedience say to God?

What great privilege can we experience because we obey God, and what evidence of this kind of relationship do you see in the lives of exemplary biblical disciples?

4. In his second letter to the church at Corinth, the Apostle Paul described vividly what his life in service to God had been like. What suffering had he endured, and how was his ministry made possible? Read 2 Corinthians 6:4–10.

What evidence do you see in this passage of a disciple who has been molded and transformed by an abiding faith in and walk with God?

What contrasts did Paul recognize between the world's perspective and the reality he lived in as a faithful disciple of Christ?

My Next Step—Making It Personal

Everyone who wants to follow Christ must ask this question: What is my commitment to accept the high calling of Christ and live in faithful obedience to God's commands—including participation in Christ's suffering? Jesus' disciples and the Apostle Paul had an answer for that. So did Richard and Sabina, Raymond and Susanna, and countless other faithful disciples of Christ who live today or have gone before us. This question deserves our most diligent study of God's Word and thoughtful consideration of who we are, who God wants us to become, and how deeply we love our Lord and Savior.

How willing are we to take on the mission—the risk and shame, the blessing and honor—God has given to us?

To what extent do we believe Christ is worthy of any risk we may face in serving him?

How deep is our commitment to God to die to ourselves, take up our cross, and follow him daily?

When we think of bearing a cross for Christ, we often think in terms of the visible, physical realm of actions, tasks, opposition, and persecution. But experiencing grief, pain, fear, and loss are part of being a living sacrifice for Christ, too. Just ask Susanna Koh, Sabina Wurmbrand, Gracia Burnham, Semse Aydin, Anita Smith, Rashin Soodmand, and thousands of other biblical disciples.

Other than having to endure five hours of police interrogation when she went to them to help find her husband, Susanna Koh was not physically afflicted by her persecutors. But she suffered deep loss because of her husband's mysterious and unsolved disappearance. For weeks she suffered fear and intimidation, panic attacks, and loss of sleep and appetite. And when she finally saw the video of her husband's abduction, she couldn't breathe. She continues to live with the pain of not knowing who took her husband or what they did with him. Suffering on the inside that we can't see is just as real as the suffering we can see.

Nevertheless, we have a God who deeply loves us and has promised to be with everyone who obeys and serves him. When we face heartbreaking sacrifices, he who abides with us and is intimately acquainted with our sufferings will prove himself faithful and trustworthy. Susanna can look at her suffering and say, "Keep your eyes on Jesus," because he is the one who does the "deep work" in our lives. He is the one who produces character and perseverance in the midst of our suffering. He is the one who writes the good ending to our life story. For Susanna, that is worth every sacrifice. "That's what I want to see for my own life and for others who are suffering," she says.

What will you risk to make serving Christ your highest priority?

As you count the cost of sacrificial obedience to Christ, consider the following accounts of Paul, who served him through great sacrifice and found him sufficient for the journey:

> Blessed be the God and Father of our Lord Jesus Christ, the Father of mercies and God of all comfort, who comforts us in all our affliction, so that we may be able to comfort those who are in any affliction, with the comfort with which we ourselves are comforted by God. For as we share abundantly in Christ's sufferings, so through Christ we share abundantly in comfort too.... For we do not want you to be unaware, brothers, of the affliction we experienced in Asia. For we were so utterly burdened beyond our strength that we despaired of life itself. Indeed, we felt that we had received the sentence of death. But that was to make us rely not on ourselves but on God who raises the dead.
>
> 2 Corinthians 1:3–5, 8–9

I was appointed a preacher and apostle and
teacher, which is why I suffer as I do. But I am
not ashamed, for I know whom I have believed,
and I am convinced that he is able to guard until
that day what has been entrusted to me.

2 Timothy 1:11–12

To what extent does the burden of that sacrifice keep you from
taking your next step toward becoming a biblical disciple?

What next step—what obedience despite risk—will you commit to take as a follower of Christ?

Session 5

OBEDIENT FORGIVENESS

But I say to you who hear, Love your enemies, do good to those who
hate you, bless those who curse you, pray for those who abuse you.
To one who strikes you on the cheek, offer the other also, and from
one who takes away your cloak do not withhold your tunic either.
Give to everyone who begs from you, and from one who takes away
your goods do not demand them back. And as you wish that others
would do to you, do so to them.... But love your enemies, and do
good, and lend, expecting nothing in return, and your reward will
be great, and you will be sons of the Most High, for he is kind to
the ungrateful and the evil. Be merciful, even as your Father is
merciful. Judge not, and you will not be judged; condemn not, and
you will not be condemned; forgive, and you will be forgiven.

Luke 6:27–31, 35–37

Introduction

If we have been followers of Christ for any length of time, we likely have asked for and received forgiveness from God many times. But how well do we function on the giving end of forgiveness? When others have wronged us and caused us to suffer, are we quick to love and forgive? Let's take a brief self-test:

How easy is it to forgive someone who expresses anger, criticism, hostility, or mockery toward us after a misunderstanding or disagreement?

How easy is it to forgive someone who lies to us or makes false accusations that assault our character or harm our reputation?

How easy is it to forgive someone who denies us or our loved ones opportunities for justice, education, safety, or employment?

How easy is it to forgive someone who takes what belongs to us—through burglary, fraud, illegal confiscation, or destruction?

How easy is it to forgive someone who harms, maims, tortures, or kills our loved ones?

Forgiving others for wrongdoing against us is often a struggle. Even if we know it is the right thing to do, we may not want to do it. Instead, we may withhold forgiveness if the other person hasn't confessed wrongdoing or asked for forgiveness.

To what extent do we feel justified in making excuses or putting conditions on our forgiveness?

If we do not forgive those who have wronged us, how might we impact the person who has offended us? How would it impact our growth in biblical discipleship?

Video Discussion

Watch the video for Session 5 and discuss the following questions with your class or group.

1. Let's talk about what it might have been like for Sabina to deal with the reality of what her entire family as well as friends suffered during and after the pogrom of Iasi.

How do you think Sabina suffered with the knowledge of what happened to her family? How might it have affected her trust in God?

In our previous study session, we discussed the "deep work" that Susanna Koh identified. What "deep work" did Sabina have to do so she could lovingly forgive Borila, the Nazi soldier who killed her family?

2. Ronnie and Anita knew that engaging in relationships in Benghazi could be dangerous. Still, they accepted the risk, and all seemed to be going well—until the day Ronnie was killed.

In relationship to her husband's death, what did Anita initially pray for that began a process that led her to pray for her husband's murderers and eventually to forgive them?

For Anita, forgiveness in the midst of her suffering did not come instantly; she had to fight for it. Through continually praying for Christ to be made known and magnified through the situation, she not only learned to forgive, but she also found joy and hope for the future.

When forgiveness is difficult, like Anita experienced, how can we ask God to help us? What can he help us become?

If we pray for Christ to be magnified and known through our suffering, or start praying for those who have harmed us to know the love of Jesus, what do we expect God will do in our hearts and our willingness to obey him? What will he do in the hearts and minds of those who have caused our suffering?

When have you seen God respond to such prayers in a powerful way? What happened as a result?

3. In light of the conversation between Richard and Borila, would you have expected the love and forgiveness Sabina showed to Borila to prove to him that God is real?

Why do you think her actions toward him made such an impact?

4. After her husband, Ronnie, was murdered in Benghazi, Anita had to decide where she stood and how she would respond. She had been deeply influenced by Richard Wurmbrand's book, *Tortured for Christ,* and remembered how Richard and Sabina forgave and pressed on in their discipleship journey. At the time, she thought, *That's not something I could ever do.* Yet after Ronnie died, Anita did what she couldn't have imagined—she willingly prayed for and forgave his killers.

Such prayers don't come instantly. They come as followers of Christ focus their hearts and minds on God's eternal perspective. That focus comes from praying for God's will to be done, abiding in God's Word, and taking on the character of Christ. Prayerfully consider the following passages that reflect the heart of a biblical disciple: Matthew 5:6–11; Matthew 5:43–44; 1 John 4:8–12, 19–20. With these passages in mind, answer the following questions:

Who do you have a hard time praying for, and why?

How will you pray for God to embolden you with his love so that you can love that person with the love of God?

How will you pray for that person to seek God and come to repentance?

What do you need to confess to God about your feelings toward this person so that you yourself can forgive?

5. Forgiveness is a powerful action. Through this video, what have you realized about how Christ works in us to release the power of forgiveness that can bring the lost to Christ?

How would you describe the importance of learning to forgive during our growth as biblical disciples?

In what ways does forgiving others change us?

Stepping Forward in the Power of God's Word

Reflect on these passages of Scripture throughout the week.

Let all bitterness and wrath and anger and clamor and slander be put away from you, along with all malice. Be kind to one another, tenderhearted, forgiving one another, as God in Christ forgave you.

Ephesians 4:31–32

Put on then, as God's chosen ones, holy and beloved, compassionate hearts, kindness, humility, meekness, and patience, bearing with one another and, if one has a complaint against another, forgiving each other; as the Lord has forgiven you, so you also must forgive. And above all these put on love, which binds everything together in perfect harmony.

Colossians 3:12–14

For Additional Reflection

Offering forgiveness for persecution that we experience against us or our loved ones is usually considered an abnormal human response. That persecution could include imprisonment, beatings, intimidation, kidnapping, torture or murder. Such forgiveness is like running toward danger rather than away from it. It is like loving your enemies. It is like counting the cost and plunging forward because the cause of Christ is worth it. For exemplary biblical disciples, such abnormal actions become the norm.

What enables a person to live this way? It's simple: Jesus loves us beyond measure, and he sacrificed everything for our redemption. He commands those who follow him to do the same for others. And love for our Savior compels us to obey faithfully.

God is the source of the love and forgiveness we demonstrate in life. The path of forgiveness is not easy, and the journey requires all that we are capable of giving. But as we grow in the knowledge of God's Word and obey him faithfully, God accomplishes a miracle in our hearts and minds. When we offer deep and sincere forgiveness, we—both the one offering forgiveness and the recipient—are surprised. We become participants in a distinctly supernatural act with eternal consequences.

1. Our understanding of God's forgiveness begins with one fundamental characteristic that defines God, his relationship and interaction with humankind, and the motivation of biblical disciples. What characteristic of God must we know and practice above all else? Read 1 John 4:7–10.

What has God done to demonstrate his love for all humanity? Read John 3:16–17.

In what ways does the love of God differ from our typical understanding of what love is?

Why is the source of our love important?

2. We generally like to think of ourselves as good people who deserve a good life and good standing in the eyes of others.

However, before we were reconciled with God, what did he consider us to be? Read Romans 5:7–11.

Did you ever think of yourself as the "enemy" of God? Do you think most people who are lost in sin think of themselves as God's enemies? Explain your answer.

In what ways does our recognition of the difference between our human view of ourselves and God's view impact how we express God's love and forgiveness to the lost?

In what ways does this key difference in perspective impact our expectations of how the lost will respond to what we tell them about God's love and forgiveness?

3. Motivated by his boundless love, God has offered redemption and forgiveness of sin to all people. What is his big plan that he wants us to accomplish? Read Ephesians 1:7–10.

What do the phrases "riches of his grace," "lavished upon us," "sympathize with our weaknesses," "throne of grace," and "receive mercy" communicate to you about how much God loves us and wants us to experience his love? Read Hebrews 4:14–16.

In what ways do you think God's gracious love can shape our interaction with those who have wronged us and our willingness to forgive them?

4. God's amazing plan to redeem and unite all things in him will be accomplished through the faithful, obedient service of biblical disciples who love him. During his ministry on earth, Jesus was asked which commandment was most important. He answered: "Love the Lord your God with all your heart and with all your soul and with all your mind and with all your strength" (Mark 12:30).

How does John 15:12–13 describe the standard of love that Jesus commands us to demonstrate?

What needs to die in us so that we can love as Jesus loves? Read Galatians 2:20.

5. In John 13:12–17, Jesus presents himself as an example for his disciples to follow. We often think of this passage in terms of how followers of Christ are to treat one another, which is entirely

appropriate. But if we, as servants of Jesus, think of all that he has done for us, what kind of example has he set for us in terms of love and forgiveness for all people?

If we belong to God, we have the privilege and calling to be like him. What does Jesus' model of love and forgiveness look like? Read Luke 6:35–36; Ephesians 5:1–2; Colossians 3:12–14.

In what ways do you think these qualities and life practices help us love and forgive those who have wronged or harmed us?

How challenging will it be for us to learn to live, love, and forgive according to Jesus' example? For instance, how well do mercy, humility, compassion, and kindness characterize our attitudes and relationships?

My Next Step—Making It Personal

During his life on earth, Jesus taught his disciples how to live for him in all circumstances, even when they were under the pressure of persecution. As we've learned, it was not uncommon for him to use himself as an example of how to live and serve God. Perhaps the most profound example occurred when Jesus hung on the cross. Although he was suffering beyond comprehension, Jesus remained focused on God's eternal perspective. As the soldiers mocked him and cast lots to divide his garments among them, he said, "Father, forgive them, for they know not what they do" (Luke 23:34).

Offering forgiveness to one's persecutors when one is dying is unheard of. Yet that is what Christ's love does. A heart overflowing with love and forgiveness provides a unique perspective in the midst of persecution. Richard's perspective after he had been imprisoned and beaten was "thankful to be among the beaten rather than those who beat." Another time, he encouraged Sabina to think of their persecutors not as enemies to be feared but as souls to be won for Christ.

Forgiving others because God has forgiven us is a necessary practice for anyone who would become a biblical disciple. We have explored some of what the Bible teaches about God's love and forgiveness. When it comes to applying that teaching in everyday life, though, we sometimes better understand what something *is* by considering what it is *not*. Sabina's conversation with Elsa, an old Party member and Secret Police officer who fell victim to a Party purge and was now a fellow prisoner, reveals the darkness of life without forgiveness. Her story helps us understand why forgiveness is essential in the life of a biblical disciple:

I said, "Elsa, do you still believe in the Party?"

"Certainly," she replied. "I haven't changed my beliefs. My arrest was all a mistake."

"Nor has my arrest altered my faith. In fact, it's stronger. I want to tell people what a friend they have in Jesus."

"You'll get the whole cell punished. I don't intend to suffer for you and your God. Anyway, he hasn't helped you much."

"This God you so dislike," I wondered, "what sort of being is he...What is your idea of God?"

"Ha!" She relished the chance for a textbook reply. God was the fanatic who wouldn't let science tell the truth. The patron of the exploiters of the proletariat. With the money they squeezed, they built churches to him. He blesses weapons of destruction on both sides.

I said, "What you call God is certainly very unlovable. The God I love is another. He shared the poverty of the workers. He was brought up among the oppressed. He fed the hungry and healed the sick. He teaches love. He died for us ..."

"Love!" Her face cracked. "What good is that? To me, anyway. I tell you, I'm all hate! If you knew how I loathed those treacherous comrades who put me here. I wish them in hell! I gave my whole life to the Party, and this is what they do to me." She bowed her head. There was a hint of a tear in her eye. It didn't seem that there was anything I could do at that moment.

"Praying? Forgive them, Father?" She hissed the words. "I don't accept forgiveness; it's lies." She began to weep.

"It's all the same," she sobbed. "If the Yanks come, I'll be hanged. If the Communists stay, I'm stuck in jail. Forgiveness!" The tears ran.

The Pastor's Wife

God's love is so vast that he does not want even one of his lost children to live in such despair. He does not wish "that any should perish, but that all should reach repentance" (2 Peter 3:9). As a result, he is faithful to forgive every sin, purify every heart, and lift the head of everyone who comes to him with a heart of repentance. The power of his forgiveness makes each of us a new creation.

No matter what terrible sins have been committed against us, they have been more painful to God than to us, yet he lovingly, unfailingly forgives. If we are Christ-like ambassadors of his kingdom, how can the despair of a sinner hopelessly bound in the darkness of sin not break our hearts? How can it not stir the love of God within us to forgive and set the prisoner free?

We are blessed that God gives us an alternative to a life of despair and hate that is found in the ability to love others as he has loved us.

Elsa could not imagine such love. Sabina, on the other hand, knew there was hope for her in Christ. How did Sabina follow the example of a faithful biblical disciple set out in 2 Timothy 2:24–26?

> And the Lord's servant must not be quarrelsome but kind to everyone, able to teach, patiently enduring evil, correcting his opponents with gentleness. God may perhaps grant them repentance leading to a knowledge of the truth, and they may come to their senses and escape from the snare of the devil, after being captured by him to do his will.

Who do you know who desperately needs God's love and forgiveness?

How has God put you in a place to share his love and forgiveness with this person?

What challenges and risks might you face when you reach out to this person? Are they worth the cause of Christ?

In what specific ways might you demonstrate God's unfailing love and forgiveness to this person?

Session 6

Fruitfulness: The Result of Faithfulness

You did not choose me, but I chose you and appointed you that you should go and bear fruit and that your fruit should abide, so that whatever you ask the Father in my name, he may give it to you. These things I command you, so that you will love one another.

John 15:16–17

Introduction

A faithful and obedient follower of Christ is supposed to bear spiritual fruit, but what does that actually mean?

What does fruitfulness in the daily life of a biblical disciple look like?

What might be the priorities, attitudes, and actions of fruitful disciples?

As we consider the topic of bearing spiritual fruit, what questions or frustrations surface regarding being a fruitful disciple?

How might a person who is just beginning to walk as a disciple of Jesus be fruitful?

When the fruit of your obedience becomes evident, how do you guard your heart against the sin of pride?

At some point in becoming biblical disciples, we will encounter challenges. We will face opposition or persecution for speaking out about our faith. Richard and Sabina's obedience to meet their neighbors for the sake of Christ led to smashed jam, rudeness, and even ethnic slander. But they were willing to pay that price so they could be a part of God's plan to see others experience faith in Christ. Maryam and Marziyeh were just two ordinary girls who placed New Testaments in different parts of Iran—and distributed tens of thousands of Bibles.

How does each of these examples inspire your own understanding of obedience?

What price were each of these exemplary biblical disciples willing to pay?

Video Discussion

Watch the video for Session 6 and discuss the following questions with your class or group.

1. One notable characteristic of Richard and Sabina was their dedication to obey and serve Christ, no matter the cost. As they walked out their faith over time, their circumstances changed dramatically, yet the faithful pursuit of their mission to tell others

about Christ did not. As their knowledge of Christ and his will for their lives grew, their obedience increased to match, or even exceed, their knowledge. Likewise, Maryam and Marziyeh had every instruction they needed from God's Word to walk in obedience and act in God's power (Acts 1:8).

In what specific ways does your obedience match, or exceed, your knowledge of Christ's instructions for you?

What is something specific you know God has instructed you to do that you have yet to obey?

How can you close your own knowledge/obedience gap related to that instruction?

2. What planted seed led Maryam to learn about Jesus and place her faith in him?

We do not know who planted that gospel seed or when, but how do you think the person who planted it would respond after learning the result?

How difficult do you think it would be to plant seeds consistently yet not know if they ever grow to maturity and bear fruit?

3. Maryam and Marziyeh read the Bible, prayed earnestly, and sought direction for how they could obey God's command to be his witnesses. In their country, all faiths other than Islam are severely persecuted. As unmarried women, they had to adapt to restricted freedoms and limited opportunities to interact with other people. What do you think of the plan they pursued? Is it a plan you might have thought of? Why or why not?

How dangerous do you think it was for them to serve God by putting New Testaments into mailboxes night after night?

How might you react upon learning that your seed-planting labor made such an impact for Christ that it drew the attention of your country's government, which is hostile to Christ and his followers?

4. We have far less control of external circumstances than we might like to admit. For Maryam and Marziyeh, being arrested and imprisoned ended their Bible distribution. They lived under terribly abusive conditions. They could do nothing short of denying Christ to regain their freedom. What did they realize about serving God in their new surroundings?

What specific things did they do in order to remain faithful, obedient, and fruitful during that time?

What was the result of their obedience while imprisoned?

5. When we come to Christ and faithfully live out our commitment as obedient, biblical disciples, we truly become new creations. We are no longer the same people we once were. We become more like Christ, and that identity sets us apart from those who do not know him. How does a Christ-like identity impact the world? Read Matthew 5:14–16.

What eternal fruit does our identity in Christ yield?

What exciting news did Paul share with his fellow believers about the fruit his suffering produced? Read Philippians 1:12–14.

Paul did not report that anyone had yet come to Christ through his witness, but in what ways was his life still bearing eternal fruit for God's kingdom?

Toward the end of his life, how did Paul feel about the way he had lived out his discipleship journey and what awaited him in heaven? Read 2 Timothy 4:5–8.

In light of what Paul writes, what challenges and what hope can a biblical disciple anticipate?

Stepping Forward in the Power of God's Word

Reflect on these passages of Scripture throughout the week.

> And so, from the day we heard, we have not ceased to pray for you, asking that you may be filled with the knowledge of his will in all spiritual wisdom and understanding, so as to walk in a manner worthy of the Lord, fully pleasing to him: bearing fruit in every good work and increasing in the knowledge of God; being strengthened with all power, according to his glorious might, for all endurance and patience with joy; giving thanks to the Father, who has qualified you to share in the inheritance of the saints in light. He has delivered us from the domain of darkness and transferred us to the kingdom of his beloved Son, in whom we have redemption, the forgiveness of sins.
>
> Colossians 1:9–14

For God is my witness, how I yearn for you all with the affection of Christ Jesus. And it is my prayer that your love may abound more and more, with knowledge and all discernment, so that you may approve what is excellent, and so be pure and blameless for the day of Christ, filled with the fruit of righteousness that comes through Jesus Christ, to the glory and praise of God.

I want you to know, brothers, that what has happened to me has really served to advance the gospel, so that it has become known throughout the whole imperial guard and to all the rest that my imprisonment is for Christ. And most of the brothers, having become confident in the Lord by my imprisonment, are much more bold to speak the word without fear.

Philippians 1:8–14

For Additional Reflection

Exemplary biblical disciples who live with eternity in mind don't come ready-made. Richard and Sabina, for example, became believers with a hunger to know more about God. They then became disciples who faithfully studied his Word. They hungered to know the Word deeply and lived it out obediently. They assessed the risks associated with following Christ and made their choice.

Through sacrificial obedience in making Christ known to the lost, Richard and Sabina became exemplary biblical disciples.

Their faithfulness in serving God cost them years in prisons and labor camps. Their faithfulness to know God and his Word prepared them to stand against opposition and persecution. Their faithfulness to obey God's commands yielded eternal fruit that still honors God and brings encouragement to others who walk the journey of biblical discipleship. Faithfulness and fruitfulness go hand in hand. A life that yields eternal fruitfulness doesn't come naturally to us, but as followers of Christ, we have the love, grace, wisdom, and power to walk out our discipleship journey to the glory of God.

1. Before Jesus Christ left his disciples on earth, he met with them on a mountaintop in Galilee and taught them how to continue living as his disciples:

> Go therefore and make disciples of all nations, baptizing them in the name of the Father and of the Son and of the Holy Spirit, teaching them to observe all that I have commanded you. And behold, I am with you always, to the end of the age.
>
> Matthew 28:19–20

Their mission was clear: Go out into the world and teach others so that greater numbers of faithful, obedient disciples will accomplish God's work in the world. But how would they fulfill this mission? They had been with Jesus and believed what he taught, but they had little experience teaching others. And Jesus had warned them that some people would reject their message and hate and persecute them. How could Jesus help them if he wasn't physically with them? The parable Jesus told about the vine and the branches helps us understand how Jesus is with us and makes it possible to live a fruitful life. Read John 15:4–11.

In this parable, Jesus compares himself to a vine that gives life to its branches, enabling them to produce fruit. What do you think *abiding* in Jesus looks like, and why is abiding in Jesus essential if we desire to live out our calling and bear eternal fruit?

How do you think biblical disciples abide in Christ? What does abiding in Christ provide for us?

Think for a moment about how you live day to day. To what extent do you think we believe Jesus' declaration that "apart from me, you can do nothing"? Give some examples of what we do that would either prove our belief or cause us to question it.

How seriously do we consider the consequences to our discipleship journey if we do not abide in Jesus (see v. 6)?

This passage conveys a weighty message, but what wonderful promise accompanies it?

Why is it important for love and joy to be a part of the conversation about discipleship and eternal fruit?

2. Confidence of our success in what we do feels good. When we are successful in our work, we may gain a raise or be able to expand our business. Success in creative or athletic endeavors may be recognized through awards and medals. Healthy and satisfying relationships with family and friends indicate success on a personal level. But what indicates success on a spiritual level? How can we know we are bearing fruit as God intends?

Sometimes, the answer to this question is clear. When people recognize their sinful state, seek forgiveness, and choose Jesus as their Lord and Savior, we see the fruit. However, the fruit of service to our Lord is not always visible. Maryam and Marziyeh, for example, labored for three years in the darkness of night distributing Bibles, always at risk and never knowing if their obedience was fruitful. Do you think they might have been discouraged in continuing their work? Why or why not?

How might you have felt about your fruitfulness (or lack thereof) if you had a similar experience?

What do you think sustains biblical disciples who have labored for years without visible evidence that their obedience was fruitful?

Regardless of physical evidence, what does God's Word assure to us regarding our faithful obedience to Christ? Read 1 Corinthians 15:58.

In what ways does this assurance give you confidence and encouragement to press on in your discipleship journey?

What do we know about the fruitfulness of planting seeds and making God's Word known in the world? Read Isaiah 55:10–11.

3. We've learned about the biblical foundation for obedient service to Christ that leads to eternal fruitfulness. Take a few minutes to talk about ideas for everyday, practical actions that will help us live out our faith in ways that will yield eternal fruit by…

…anchoring our lives in the Word of God

…counting the cost of our obedience while knowing opposition will come

…demonstrating that our obedience matches our knowledge

…boldly sharing Christ's love and forgiveness to the lost

My Next Step—Making It Personal

Being a fruitful disciple always comes at a price. The risk of loving Christ enough to obey him and become a faithful witness of his sacrificial love requires something of us—our time, our possessions, our energy, our safety, or even our lives. In John 12:24–26, Jesus says, "Truly, truly, I say to you, unless a grain of wheat falls into the earth and dies, it remains alone; but if it dies, it bears much fruit. Whoever loves his life loses it, and whoever hates his life in this world will keep it for eternal life. If anyone serves me, he must follow me; and where I am, there will my servant be also. If anyone serves me, the Father will honor him."

How costly is it for you to be a fruitful disciple? Read John 15:12–14, 16–21.

What price are you willing to pay to live out your commitment to Christ and produce the eternal fruit of biblical discipleship?

When we participate in God's redemptive work on earth by walking faithfully in obedience to Christ's commands, how priceless is the reward we receive for eternity? Read Philippians 3:7–8.

Living in light of eternity changes our perspective on everything. To what extent does your labor for eternal fruit direct your steps as you walk out your discipleship journey?

Knowing that sacrificial discipleship can be extremely difficult, what solace did Jesus provide for the journey, and how does that help you endure? Read John 16:33.

What does obedience to God's call on your life look like for you personally? Be specific.

What is the next costly step you are willing to take in your discipleship journey?

Even when Maryam and Marziyeh were confined in notorious Evin Prison, they continued to pursue the work to which God called them. They knew God had a purpose for them in that place, and they considered it a privilege to walk in obedience to him. In the midst of great darkness, they maintained their witness of God's love.

"Even in such a place we can love one another," they said. Food was scarce, and others kept whatever they could for themselves—just to survive. To the amazement of their cellmates, Maryam and Marziyeh shared what they had with others. Even though their cellmates called them "dirty Christians," Maryam and Marziyeh listened to their stories and prayed for them. The two women lived with eternity in mind.

It takes more than human kindness to make the sacrifices Maryam and Marziyeh lovingly made in prison. It takes God-empowered courage to continue telling others about Jesus and praying for them while in prison in Iran because of Christ! What does Acts 1:8 reveal about the source of their love, strength, and resolve to remain faithful to Christ during their time in prison?

> But you will receive power when the Holy Spirit
> has come upon you, and you will be my witnesses
> in Jerusalem and in all Judea and Samaria, and to
> the end of the earth.
>
> Acts 1:8

In what ways did Maryam and Marziyeh live out the teaching of Romans 5:1–5?

> Therefore, since we have been justified by faith,
> we have peace with God through our Lord Jesus
> Christ. Through him we have also obtained access
> by faith into this grace in which we stand, and we

rejoice in hope of the glory of God. Not only that, but we rejoice in our sufferings, knowing that suffering produces endurance, and endurance produces character, and character produces hope, and hope does not put us to shame, because God's love has been poured into our hearts through the Holy Spirit who has been given to us.

Romans 5:1–5

In what ways does their example encourage you to be an obedient disciple, faithful to your calling to make Christ known?

What assurance does this passage of Scripture provide for you when facing the storms that will test your faith?

What steps of sacrificial obedience will you take to make Christ known to the lost?

10 WAYS TO PRAY
FOR PERSECUTED CHRISTIANS

The first request of our persecuted brothers and sisters is "Pray for us!" As you spend time in prayer for our persecuted Christian family, focus on these specific requests:

- Pray for persecuted Christians to sense God's presence (Heb. 13:5).
- Pray they will feel connected to the greater body of Christ (1 Cor. 12:20, 26).
- Pray they will be comforted by God when their family members are killed, injured, or imprisoned for their witness (2 Cor. 1:3–5).
- Pray they will have more opportunities to share the gospel (Col. 4:3).
- Pray for the boldness to make Christ known (Phil. 1:14).
- Pray they will forgive and love their persecutors (Matt. 5:44).
- Pray their ministry activities will remain undetected by authorities or others who wish to silence them (Acts 9:20–25).
- Pray they will rejoice in suffering (Acts 5:41).
- Pray they will be refreshed through God's Word and grow in their faith (Eph. 6:17).
- Pray they will be strengthened through the prayers of fellow believers (Jude 20–25).

About The Voice
of the Martyrs

The Voice of the Martyrs (VOM) is a nonprofit, interdenominational Christian organization that serves persecuted Christians on the world's most difficult and dangerous mission fields and brings other members of the body of Christ into fellowship with them. VOM was founded in 1967 by Pastor Richard Wurmbrand and his wife, Sabina. Richard was imprisoned 14 years in Communist Romania for his faith in Christ, and Sabina was imprisoned for three years. They were ransomed out of Romania in 1965 and soon established a global network of missions dedicated to assisting persecuted Christians.

To be inspired by the courageous faith of our persecuted brothers and sisters in Christ who are advancing the gospel in hostile areas and restricted nations, request a free subscription to VOM's award-winning monthly magazine. Visit us at vom.org, or call 800-747-0085.

To learn more about VOM's work, please contact us:

United States	vom.org
Australia	vom.com.au
Belgium	hvk-aem.be
Brazil	maisnomundo.org
Canada	vomcanada.com
Czech Republic	hlas-mucedniku.cz
Finland	marttyyrienaani.fi
Germany	verfolgte-christen.org
The Netherlands	sdok.nl
New Zealand	vom.org.nz
Poland	gpch.pl
Portugal	vozdosmartires.com
Singapore	gosheninternational.org
South Africa	persecutionsa.org
South Korea	vomkorea.kr
United Kingdom	releaseinternational.org

JOIN IN A JOURNEY TO MEET PERSECUTED CHRISTIANS.

INSPIRE YOUR FRIENDS AND FAMILY WITH STORIES FROM THE FRONTLINES!

Receive a free copy of Todd Nettleton's new book, *When Faith Is Forbidden: 40 Days on the Frontlines with Persecuted Christians*, with any donation to The Voice of the Martyrs. With any gift of $30 or more, you will receive two copies of *When Faith Is Forbidden*, one for you and one to share!

one for you and one to share!

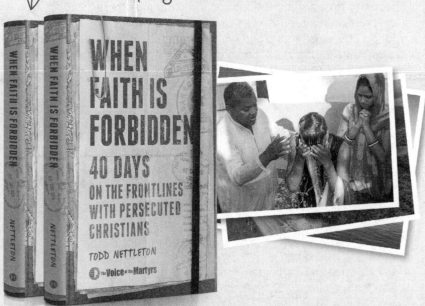

From The Voice of the Martyrs and Moody Publishers

GET A FREE COPY FOR YOUR GIFT!
vom.org/forbidden

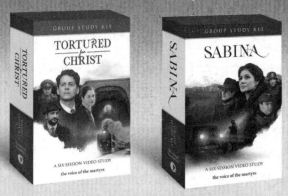